Who Was
Jacqueline Kennedy?

by Bonnie Bader

illustrated by Joseph J. M. Qiu

Penguin Workshop

For Lauren and Allie,
who are growing up to be strong women—BB

This book is dedicated to Jackie Kennedy, an
extraordinary woman—JQ

PENGUIN WORKSHOP
An Imprint of Penguin Random House LLC, New York

Text copyright © 2016 by Bonnie Bader. Illustrations copyright © 2016 by Penguin Random House LLC. All rights reserved. Published by Penguin Workshop, an imprint of Penguin Random House LLC, New York. PENGUIN and PENGUIN WORKSHOP are trademarks of Penguin Books Ltd. WHO HQ & Design is a registered trademark of Penguin Random House LLC. Printed in the USA.

Visit us online at www.penguinrandomhouse.com.

Library of Congress Control Number: 2016033769

ISBN 9780448486987 (paperback)   10 9 8 7
ISBN 9780399542428 (library binding)   10 9 8 7 6 5 4 3 2

Contents

Who Was Jacqueline Kennedy?

On May 31, 1961, a large crowd packed the streets of Paris, France. Waving American and French flags, people were waiting for the president of the United States, John F. Kennedy, and his wife, Jacqueline.

At last, the car rolled into view. The crowd roared. But they did not shout for the president. Instead, they called out, "Jackie! Jackie!"

A shy Jackie looked out the car window and waved. Seven months earlier, her husband had become the youngest person elected president of the United States. He was forty-three years old. Jackie was only thirty-one. She was unsure if she would make a good First Lady. But here she was—young and beautiful and charming—captivating the French people!

A harder test would come later. The president of France, Charles de Gaulle, did not really like anything, or anyone, who wasn't French.

The next night, Jackie got ready for a special dinner in the Kennedys' honor. She did not feel well. Her head throbbed. She did not know what to wear. Two dresses were laid out on the bed. An American designer had made one; a French designer named Hubert de Givenchy had made the other. Jackie chose the Givenchy. She was in France, so she wore something French!

Jackie smiled as she glided into the party that night. Her white gown shimmered. Gold clips sparkled in her hair.

At the long candlelit table, Jackie sat next to President de Gaulle. She charmed him with her French. She had lived in Paris for a year during college. She knew all about French art and French history. Because of Jackie, President de Gaulle turned to President Kennedy and said, "I now have more confidence in your country."

Talking to reporters back home, President Kennedy jokingly introduced himself as "the man who accompanied Jacqueline Kennedy to Paris, and I have enjoyed it."

It wasn't only the French president who was fascinated by Jackie. The whole world was. Jacqueline Kennedy had become the most famous woman on earth, yet all her life what she wanted most was privacy.

CHAPTER 1
A Rich Family

Jacqueline Lee Bouvier was born on July 28, 1929, in Southampton, New York, into a very rich family. Jackie's father, John, was handsome and full of life. His wife, Janet, was quiet and shy. She loved riding horses.

Janet and John Bouvier

The Bouviers had two homes. One was a fancy apartment on Park Avenue in Manhattan; the other was a beautiful mansion on Long Island. That was where the family spent summers. It was called Lasata, which was said to be a Native American name for "place of peace."

But the Bouvier home was not peaceful. John (usually called Jack) and Janet argued a lot. Janet was practical. Jack liked to have fun and spend money.

Soon after Jacqueline was born, her father lost most of his money. On October 29, 1929, the stock market crashed. It was the start of the Great Depression. Many people lost their jobs and homes. The Bouviers were not hit nearly as hard; still, the family had to move to a smaller apartment. Janet's father owned the building and let them live there without paying rent.

From her father, Jacqueline got a nickname— Jackie. From her mother came Jackie's love of horses. When Jackie was just a year old, Janet put her on a horse and began teaching her to ride.

Jackie on horseback
at age five

The Crash of 1929

The date the stock market crashed, October 29, 1929, is known as Black Tuesday. Buying a stock is like buying a "share" or a part of a company. When a company you have stock in makes money, so do you. When the company loses money, you do, too. In the stock market, prices rise and fall every day.

On Black Tuesday, the stock market fell and lost $14 billion. The total loss that week was $30 billion. As the news of the crash spread, people rushed to banks to take out their money. But the banks did not have enough cash to give out to everyone. Many banks closed. Other businesses did, too. People lost their jobs and their homes. By 1933, many children living in the United States did not have enough to eat. The Great Depression lasted until the end of 1939.

On March 3, 1933, Jackie's sister, Caroline Lee, was born. Caroline, who everyone called Lee, was more like the girls' father—outgoing and daring.

Jackie was more like their mother. Besides horses, she loved books, and by the age of five, Jackie was reading on her own. She loved Mowgli from Rudyard Kipling's *The Jungle Book*, and the adventures of Robin Hood. Her mother wondered if Jackie might grow up to become a writer.

In 1935, Jackie enrolled at Miss Chapin's, an all-girls school in New York City. She got top grades but was also a bit of a troublemaker. Once, Jackie smeared face cream on the school's toilet seats! She said she had been bored and just wanted to have a little fun.

At home, Jackie's parents fought more than
ever. Soon they decided to separate. Jack moved
into a hotel. On the weekends, Jackie and
Lee visited their father. They loved spending
time with him—they visited the Bronx Zoo,

took horse and buggy rides in Central Park, and
went to restaurants.

It must have hurt her deeply that her parents
were not living together. But Jackie did not show
it. She kept her feelings to herself.

John Vernou Bouvier Jr.

Besides her father, Jackie was very close to her grandfather Bouvier, whom she called Grampy Jack. They talked about history and current events. They wrote poetry together.

When Jackie was ten, her parents tried to get back together. But they still fought. Jack drank heavily, which was a big problem. In time, the marriage was over for good.

The Bouviers were Catholic, and the Catholic Church does not approve of divorce. Friends and even some relatives made mean comments to Jackie about her parents' decision. But Jackie did not listen. She tuned them out. She withdrew more into herself.

The one place she felt free was riding her horse, Danseuse. By the time she was eleven, Jackie had won several riding awards. Jackie also enjoyed ballet class and taking French lessons. And she loved going to her family's beach house, where she could listen to the waves crashing on the shore.

Although Jack was no longer living with his daughters, he remained very important to them. He bought the girls fancy clothes and took them on trips. He did not set as many rules as their mother did. It was easier for Jackie and Lee to be with their father.

The girls competed for Jack's attention, but Jackie was his favorite. She even looked like her father, with dark hair and eyes, and a big, wide smile. Jack explained to her how to dress and act. He thought a woman should be mysterious, never revealing too much about herself. Jackie remembered this all her life.

In June 1942, just before Jackie was thirteen, Janet married Hugh Auchincloss. Not only did Jackie now have a stepfather, she gained two

Hugh Auchincloss

stepbrothers, Yusha and Tommy, and a stepsister, Nina. Janet and Hugh also had two children together.

Jackie and Lee called their stepfather "Uncle Hughdie." Uncle Hughdie was very rich. He had two homes, one in McLean, Virginia, and one in Newport, Rhode Island. The home in Rhode Island, called Hammersmith Farm, was one of Newport's famous "cottages." But Hammersmith was no ordinary cottage—there were three large homes on the property, which were called the Castle, the Palace, and the Windmill.

Janet and her daughters moved to Virginia with Uncle Hughdie, and Jackie attended Holton-Arms, another all-girls school. Although her home life was now more stable, Jackie kept even more to herself. Often, instead of going out with friends, she stayed in her room reading and writing poetry.

Holton-Arms

At fifteen, Jackie was sent to Miss Porter's, an all-girls boarding school in Farmington, Connecticut. Besides the usual subjects, the school taught students how to act like proper ladies who would make good housewives. Jackie followed the rules—most of the time. She was a good student and became editor of the school newspaper.

When Jackie graduated, she wrote in the yearbook that her goal was "not to become a housewife." She applied to college and was accepted at Vassar College. Jackie could not wait for a new chapter of her life to begin. Jacqueline Bouvier had an exciting future in mind for herself!

CHAPTER 2
A Thirst for Knowledge

Jackie started at Vassar College, a women's college in Poughkeepsie, New York, in September 1947. She took classes in drawing, painting, literature, history, and religion. In her favorite class she read the great plays of William Shakespeare.

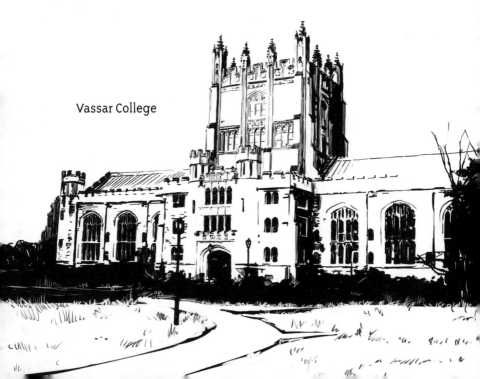

Vassar College

Sadly, halfway through her freshman year, Grampy Jack died. With money that he left her, Jackie took a summer trip to Europe with two friends.

Jackie loved every place she visited, especially Paris. In fact, her friends had a hard time getting her to leave. Jackie vowed she would be back.

True to her word, Jackie studied in Paris during her junior year. She lived with a French family in a small apartment that had no central heating. Sometimes to stay warm, Jackie wore several sweaters, woolen stockings, and earmuffs!

One cold day, Jackie wanted to take a nice warm bath. She turned up the temperature on the water heater so high that the heater exploded and broke the window. This was especially bad since the entire family shared one bathroom! Jackie was so embarrassed.

In Paris, Jackie took walks along the Seine River, ate at sidewalk cafés, and visited art galleries and jazz clubs. With a feeling of independence—a new feeling for her—Jackie visited small towns in the beautiful French countryside. Jackie later said that she enjoyed that year in Paris more than any other in her life. She said that she "learned not to be ashamed of a real hunger for knowledge, something I had always tried to hide." She came home with a love for Europe that never left her.

In order to be closer to her family in Virginia, Jackie spent her final year of college at George Washington University in Washington, DC.

One day, her mother saw an ad in *Vogue*, a fashion magazine. It was for a writing contest open to college seniors. The grand prize was six months in Paris and six months working at the magazine in

New York City. Immediately, Jackie entered the contest, and she won!

But Uncle Hughdie did not want Jackie to accept the prize. He worried that Jackie might never return from Paris. He convinced Janet that it wasn't a good idea, and a very disappointed Jackie had to turn down the prize.

Instead, Uncle Hughdie sent Jackie and her sister, Lee, to Europe for the summer. Although he was very rich, the trip was far from fancy.

The girls traveled third class on the ship across the ocean. Jackie tried again and again to sneak into the first-class area, but always got caught.

Soon the summer came to an end, and Jackie returned home. What was Jackie to do now? Settle down and get married like most of the young women she knew? No. Jackie was determined to find an interesting job.

CHAPTER 3
JFK

It was unusual in the 1950s for a rich young woman to work. But Jackie was not a typical rich young woman.

Her first job was at the *Washington Times-Herald* newspaper answering phones and filing papers.

Then a position as "the Inquiring Photographer" opened up. "Inquiring" means asking questions. Right away, Jackie applied for the job, telling the editor that she knew how to use a camera, even though she didn't. She got the job and then signed up for a photography class!

On the job, Jackie stopped people on the street and asked them funny questions. She also took their photos, which were published in the paper next to their

answers. Shy, reserved Jackie was able to get people to open up, asking, "Do you think a wife should let her husband think he is smarter than she is?" or "Which First Lady would you most like to have been?"

The job was interesting, and now that school was over, Jackie could go out and enjoy herself at night. At a party, Jackie met a man from New York named John Husted. The two fell in love, and within a month, John asked Jackie to marry him. And Jackie said yes!

But Jackie lived in Washington, DC, and John lived in New York City. Also, John did not make a lot of money. That did not sit well with Jackie's mother. She believed having a lot of money was very important. In time, Jackie's engagement was called off.

Then, at a dinner party, Jackie was seated next to a handsome congressman from Massachusetts. His name was John Fitzgerald Kennedy. At thirty-five, John—nicknamed Jack—was twelve years older than Jackie. Yet they found much to talk about. They both loved history and poetry and traveling.

On July 4, 1952, Jack brought Jackie to meet his family in Hyannis Port, on Cape Cod in Massachusetts. The Kennedys were a big, outgoing Irish-Catholic family. They loved playing sports like football and softball. Everything was a contest—even conversations at the dinner table!

During her first visits, shy Jackie tried to join in, but after breaking her ankle during a touch football game, she stayed on the sidelines.

Jackie often sat on the porch chatting with Jack's father, Joseph Kennedy. He was smart and friendly. And he enjoyed Jackie's company.

Jackie and Jack's relationship became more serious. When Jackie found out that Jack, now a Massachusetts senator, packed a cold lunch in a paper bag every day, she brought hot lunches to his office. And after Dwight Eisenhower was sworn in as president, Jackie accompanied Jack to the inaugural ball. An inaugural ball is a fancy party to celebrate the day a president begins a new term.

What Is a Senator?

The United States Senate, along with the House of Representatives, makes up what is known as Congress. The job of Congress is to make and pass laws. The Senate has one hundred people—two from each state. Each term in the Senate is for six years. A senator can be elected over and over, unlike the

president, who can serve no more than two terms. To become a senator, a person has to be at least thirty years old, live in the state they want to represent, and have been a United States citizen for at least nine years.

In May 1953, Jackie traveled to England to report on the brand-new queen, twenty-three-year-old Elizabeth II. Around that time, Jack asked Jackie to marry him. But she did not answer right away. Jackie was afraid that being a wife would end her independence. She was afraid that Jack was too old for her. She was afraid that her life would be taken over by politics. And she was afraid that Jack was too independent to be happily married.

Jackie gave the marriage proposal a lot of thought. She loved John Kennedy. So, at last, she said yes. The wedding was to take place on September 12, 1953. Jackie wanted a small ceremony, but the Kennedy family did not. They wanted the wedding to be a public event, filled with friends, family, and reporters.

There was another problem. Jackie wanted her father to walk her down the aisle. Jackie's mother was very much against this idea, but Jackie won out. However, as her father was dressing for the wedding, Jackie's cousins noticed that he had been drinking. Although Jack Bouvier insisted he was okay, the cousins called Janet. Upon hearing this news, Janet forbade him to attend the wedding. Jackie was heartbroken, but kept her feelings inside. She agreed to let Uncle Hughdie take her father's place.

Outside St. Mary's Church in Newport, Rhode Island, two thousand people gathered to see the bride and groom. Jackie wore an ivory-colored, off-the-shoulder gown. Her veil trailed behind her, and she carried a bouquet of white and pink flowers.

Inside the church were six hundred guests. Sad that her father was not giving her away, Jackie blinked back tears.

After the ceremony, there was a party for over twelve hundred people. Jackie and Jack stood for over three hours to greet all their guests!

Although Jackie smiled for the pictures later, she wrote her father telling him that in her heart, he had walked her down the aisle and had been with her during her very special day.

CHAPTER 4
Politics

Before Jackie married, she didn't know much about politics. Now she was a senator's wife and wanted to learn as much as she could. So she took a course in American history at Georgetown University.

From the beginning, she took an interest in Jack's career, helping Jack practice for speeches, giving tips on how to use his hands and voice. She also translated passages from French literature for Jack to use in his addresses.

Jack began to rely on Jackie more and more. Did she trust a certain person? Would she go to an event in Jack's place? Being in front of the public wasn't something Jackie was always comfortable with. Still, she did it, and showed grace and confidence.

In October 1954, Jack underwent back surgery to correct an old injury. But the operation failed. Then, an infection set in. Doctors told Jackie that her husband was going to die. But Jackie remained strong. She did not cry. Instead, she never left Jack's bedside. She read to him and told him jokes.

Slowly, he became stronger, and six weeks later, he was operated on again. This time, the surgery was a success.

It was a happy time in the marriage. The couple liked to discuss history and politics. Jackie convinced her husband to write a book about Senate leaders he most admired. She helped with the research, took notes, and edited his writing. The book, *Profiles in Courage*, won a very important honor, the Pulitzer Prize.

In 1956, Jackie was overjoyed to learn she was pregnant. The Kennedys bought a large house, called Hickory Hill, in McLean, Virginia. There was a swimming pool, and best of all, stables! Jackie got to work fixing up the house, filling it with antique furniture. And she decorated the baby's nursery in cheerful colors.

Eight months pregnant, Jackie accompanied her husband to Chicago, Illinois, to the Democratic

National Convention. There the Democratic candidates for president and for vice president would be chosen. The election would be that November. Jack hoped he'd be nominated for vice president. It was a big disappointment when this did not happen.

Upon returning home, Jackie was tired and stressed. And she was alone. Jack had taken off for a trip to Europe after the convention. Suddenly, she felt a sharp pain in her stomach. Jackie was rushed to the hospital, where doctors tried to save the baby. But it was too late. The baby died.

Heartbroken, Jackie could no longer face living at Hickory Hill. So the Kennedys sold the house to Jack's brother and wife, Bobby and Ethel Kennedy. Always a private person, Jackie couldn't talk to her husband about her sadness. And Jack couldn't talk about it, either. He traveled a lot, often leaving Jackie alone on weekends.

The Kennedys were growing further and

further apart. Their interests were so different—Jackie loved culture and the arts, not politics. And politics was the fire that lit Jack Kennedy's life.

Then, in July 1957, Jackie's father fell gravely ill. Jackie, who was pregnant again, went to see him. But she was too late; her father had already died.

Jackie did not shed a tear at her father's funeral. Yet she gave her daughter, Caroline, who was born on November 27, 1957, the middle name Bouvier. It was to honor her beloved father, who had been such a force in her life.

One year after Caroline's birth, Jack was reelected as senator from Massachusetts. He was a popular member of Congress, and soon his hopes were set even higher. He wanted to become president.

Jack started campaigning, often with Jackie at his side. Each time Jackie was scheduled to show up for one of his speeches, the crowd doubled in size!

In the summer of 1960, Jack won the nomination as the Democratic candidate for president. Lyndon Baines Johnson, a senator from Texas, would run as his vice president.

Television in the 1960s

On September 26, 1960, John F. Kennedy debated his opponent, Vice President Richard M. Nixon. This was the first time a presidential debate was on TV. Kennedy came across as strong, smart, and handsome. Nixon looked tired and hot—he sweated a lot! Jack Kennedy's strong performance influenced the outcome of the election.

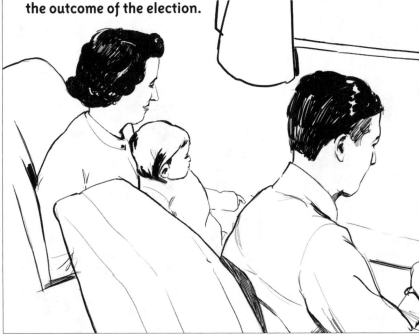

In the 1960s, most homes in America had just one television set, and it was black and white—most shows weren't televised in color until around 1965. The 1960s marked the first time people turned to television for news. For many Americans, the 1960 presidential debate was their first introduction to John F. Kennedy.

Jack's nomination caused controversy in the country. He was just forty-two years old. Many thought he was too young to be president. The president at that time, Dwight D. Eisenhower, was seventy.

Also, Jack was Roman Catholic. The country had never elected a Catholic president. Some people worried that Jack Kennedy might be influenced by the pope, the head of the Catholic Church.

Jackie, who was pregnant again, knew that her husband's campaign needed her help. She wanted to show the country that Jack was mature enough to run the country, and that his religion didn't matter. But Jackie was also scared. She did not want to put her pregnancy in danger. So she came up with an idea—she would work from home. Jackie organized eleven women in eleven states to help campaign for her husband. She wrote a newspaper column called Campaign Wife in which she discussed education issues and what she would do if she became the First Lady.

As the election drew near, Jackie understood the importance of making appearances herself. She did all she could—she gave speeches in Spanish and Italian, and visited African American

churches and attended their fundraisers. Jackie enchanted the crowds. Not only was she smart, she was glamorous. She had a simple elegant style, wearing classic, tailored suits and dresses—most often with pearls. Women across the country began to copy the Jackie "look"—down to her puffy bouffant hairdo. Jackie's smarts and style helped Jack win votes.

Tuesday, November 8, 1960, was Election Day. The whole Kennedy family—brothers, sisters, Jack's parents—gathered in Hyannis Port to wait for the results. It was a close race. Jackie

said that waiting for the votes to be counted was "the longest night in history." At last, it was clear John F. Kennedy would become the thirty-fifth president of the United States.

Jackie was only thirty-one years old. And now, she was about to become the First Lady of the United States.

CHAPTER 5
First Lady

Less than three weeks after the election, Jackie gave birth to a son, John Fitzgerald Kennedy Jr. Jackie was weak afterward and her doctors told her to take it easy. However, her life as First Lady was about to begin, and she was excited.

After John Kennedy took office on January 20, 1961, inaugural balls were held to honor him. Jackie's decision about what to wear was important. While she had campaigned for Jack, some people criticized her for wearing expensive French-designer clothes. So Jackie decided on a white satin gown with a matching cape created by American designer Oleg Cassini.

As the Kennedys were driven to the parties, Jackie smiled and waved. She looked healthy and elegant. But inside, she felt tired, nervous, and scared. Yet she did not let her feelings show.

She accompanied the new president on trips to many countries. Everywhere Jackie went, she wowed the crowds with her style, her youth, and her beauty. But she also impressed people with her intelligence.

One of the most important trips was to Vienna. There the Kennedys met Soviet leader Nikita Khrushchev and his wife in June 1961.

In the 1960s, the United States and the Soviet Union were the two superpowers of the world, and they were enemies. Jackie knew that when she met Khrushchev, she would need to be clever as well as charming. When Khrushchev bragged that the Soviet Union was ahead of the United States in the space race, Jackie ignored the remark. Instead, she asked about Strelka, one of the Soviet dogs sent

in a rocket to outer space. Khrushchev was won over. Later he sent one of Strelka's puppies to the White House as a present for Jackie.

Jackie took other trips without her husband. In March 1962, she traveled to India and Pakistan with her sister, Lee. When Jackie arrived in India, over one hundred thousand people lined the streets to see her, chanting "Ameriki Rani," which means "Queen of America."

The Cold War

The Cold War is a term used to describe the relationship between the United States and the Soviet Union after World War II. The two countries were very different. The United States was a democratic country, where the citizens were free to elect leaders. The Soviet Union was a communist country, where one party controlled the government. The people had no say.

Instead of fighting actual battles, the two countries competed for power. For example, each side piled up nuclear weapons so the other side would feel weaker.

This was known as the arms race. During the Cold War, the United States and the Soviets were also in a space race. The Soviets were first to launch a spaceship into outer space. But American astronauts were first to reach the moon in 1969.

During the trip, Jackie showed respect for
Indian culture by wearing a sari, the traditional
dress worn by Indian women. She also got to ride
an elephant. India's prime minister said that Jackie
had helped improve the friendship between India
and the United States.

Jackie showed the world that she was a charming, fashionable, and intelligent woman. Privately, she provided her husband with advice and opinions on events of the day. She was a great source of comfort when he was under pressure, often just by listening to his problems.

In a very short time, Jackie Kennedy proved to be an excellent First Lady. She was also becoming a superstar—the most famous woman in the world.

CHAPTER 6
All for the Arts

A major project for Jackie was redecorating the White House. Before the Kennedys moved in, a tour of the mansion proved to Jackie that changes were needed. She did not like what she saw. Not at all. The family rooms looked old and shabby. The White House—one of the most famous landmarks in the country—felt cold and dreary.

Very quickly, Jackie went to work. She made the private living quarters warm and homey. She wanted a comfortable place for her family out of the public eye. But beyond that, she wanted the White House to be a showplace that reflected the greatness of the country.

Jackie convinced the government to make the White House a national museum and to give her some money to fix it up. She studied the building's history and went on a treasure hunt in the White House to find items of importance.

She looked in dusty closets. She scoured the old attic. She searched the basement. What did she find? A set of china that belonged to the Lincolns. Beautiful wool rugs bought by Teddy Roosevelt. Old marble statues of George Washington and Christopher Columbus. And more.

Besides restoring the White House, Jackie persuaded famous artists to donate paintings. "Everything in the White House must have a reason for being there," Jackie said. She also worked with a gardener to redesign the now-famous White House Rose Garden.

At last, the renovation was complete. On February 14, 1962, Jackie took a television reporter on a tour of the house. A record fifty-six million people tuned in to watch the show.

Jackie spent a lot of money on the renovation.

To support the upkeep of the house, she wrote a book: *The White House: An Historic Guide.* Published in July 1962, the book sold out within the first three months. To date, close to five million copies of the book have been sold. All the money goes to the White House fund that Jackie set up.

And she showed her sense of style at dinners in the mansion. In the past, White House dinners were stuffy affairs where guests had assigned seats and sat at a huge table. Jackie was a wonderful hostess. Now guests picked their seats from pieces of paper in a bowl, and sat at small round tables of eight or ten, making conversation easier. The tables were decorated with freshly picked flowers, candles, and sparkling silverware and china.

After dinner there were performances. The famous Spanish musician Pablo Casals played his cello. Robert Frost recited poetry. Singers from the Metropolitan Opera performed. After one dinner, violinist Isaac Stern wrote to Jackie, "It would be difficult to tell you how refreshing, how heartening it is to find such serious attention and respect for the arts in the White House."

Jackie hoped to showcase the arts in Washington, DC, in an even larger way. Her dream was to create a cultural center in the capital. With support from President Kennedy, Jackie raised money. It took time and millions of dollars, but on September 8, 1971, the John F. Kennedy Center for the Performing Arts opened.

Being First Lady and constantly in the public eye was exhausting. By the beginning of 1963, Jackie was tired of world travel. Tired of raising money for the arts. And tired of politics. All she wanted was to spend time with her children. And she was pregnant again.

Jackie always wanted her children, Caroline and John, to have as normal a childhood as possible. There hadn't been young children in the White House since the early 1900s, when Teddy Roosevelt was president. The Kennedy kids were adorable, and the public couldn't get enough of them. But Jackie did not want reporters around.

When Caroline was ready for preschool, Jackie started a small one right in the White House. Children of friends and staff attended. Jackie loved being with the children and took turns teaching with the other parents. When school was out for the summer, the Kennedys took a vacation. One day, Jackie felt a sharp pain in her stomach. She was rushed to the hospital, where Patrick Bouvier Kennedy was born. But the baby was born too early and had trouble breathing. Sadly, Patrick died.

Jackie and Jack were devastated. Unlike the last time she had lost a baby, the couple became closer after this loss. Over the years, the Kennedys had their differences. There were rumors that Jack wasn't always faithful to his wife. But they were working on their marriage. Now, more than at any other time, they turned to each other for support.

CHAPTER 7
Tragedy

Three months after losing Patrick, Jack asked Jackie to travel with him to Texas. He was thinking ahead to the next presidential election, which would be in November 1964. So many people in America were wild about the Kennedy family—they were young and beautiful, and seemed like the ideal American family. Jack knew how much the public enjoyed seeing him and Jackie together. Still, he warned Jackie that this would be a tense trip. There were a lot of people in Texas who did not like his support of the civil rights movement. Perhaps Jackie's presence in Texas would help his popularity there.

Sure enough, when the couple landed in Texas, cheering crowds turned out for the Kennedys.

Kennedy and Civil Rights

John F. Kennedy opposed segregation in the United States. Yet as a senator, he actually voted against the Civil Rights Act in 1957 that would protect the right of African Americans to vote in the United States. The act passed, even without Kennedy's vote. He didn't make civil rights a top issue until the end of his presidency. On June 11, 1963, Kennedy made a televised speech outlining his civil rights bill. He hoped it would be passed by Congress within the year.

Many people shouted out Jackie's name, thrilled to catch sight of her. The Kennedys visited several Texas cities—San Antonio, Houston, and Fort Worth.

On November 22, 1963, the Kennedys arrived in Dallas. A long line of cars, called a motorcade, drove through the streets. Jackie and Jack sat in the back of a limousine with its top rolled back. The sun blazed down on thousands of people cheering and waving.

Suddenly, a shot rang out. Was someone hit? Yes, the president! Another shot rang out; the bullet hit Jack in the head. A terrified Jackie cried out, "My God, what are they doing? My God . . . they've killed my husband."

The motorcade raced to a hospital. Jackie held her husband in her arms and cried. She refused to leave his side as he was rushed into the

Lee Harvey Oswald

emergency room. But the doctors could not save him—President John F. Kennedy was dead. Later that day, the police arrested a man named Lee Harvey Oswald for assassinating the president.

The president's body was placed in a coffin and put onto a plane. But before the plane could take off, the new president had to be sworn into office. The vice president, Lyndon B. Johnson, came aboard and took the oath of office. Jackie, still wearing her blood-stained pink suit, stood at Johnson's side. Under tragic circumstances, the United States now had its thirty-sixth president.

Jackie remained composed on the plane ride back to Washington, DC. She tried to comfort her husband's staff. She started to make plans for the funeral. The one thing she couldn't bring herself to do, however, was tell her children about their father's death, so their nanny broke the news. Caroline, who was almost six, understood, but John Jr. did not. How could he? The little boy was just turning three.

The Kennedy family wanted Jack buried in Massachusetts. But Jackie insisted that her husband be buried at a military cemetery—Arlington National Cemetery. This was important to her for

two reasons. Jack had been a World War II hero, fighting in the Pacific. Also, as president he was head of all the armed forces. Jackie felt strongly that his resting place should be with other soldiers who had served the country and fought in wars.

The funeral took place on November 25, 1963.

A riderless horse followed the funeral procession down the streets of the capital. Jackie insisted on walking, rather than riding in a car. Thousands of people watched the coffin go past. Some cried; others saluted. At the steps of the church where the funeral was held, Jackie bent down and whispered something in little John's ear.

John stepped forward and saluted his father's coffin.

Throughout the day of the funeral, Jackie remained strong and composed. A British journalist later wrote, "Jacqueline Kennedy has today given her country the one thing it has always lacked, and that is majesty."

CHAPTER 8
Life Goes On

Two weeks after her husband's death, Jackie and her children moved out of the White House. At first, the family stayed in Washington, but their new home soon became a tourist attraction.

People lined up outside her house, trying to catch a glimpse of Jackie and her children. Cars and tour buses clogged the streets. Plus, the city held too many memories for Jackie. So she decided to move to New York City to start a new life.

But even far from Washington, it was hard to find privacy. Reporters and photographers constantly tried to interview Jackie and snap photos of the Kennedys. Jackie taught Caroline and John to ignore the flashing cameras. She taught them to be independent and to follow their own interests.

Still, as hard as she tried, Jackie could not forget that fateful day in Dallas. She began to rely more and more on her brother-in-law Bobby Kennedy. He became a father figure to Caroline and John Jr.

Bobby Kennedy

And Bobby relied on Jackie, too. When he ran for a Senate seat from New York, Jackie helped him with his speeches—just like she once had done for Jack. Bobby won the election on November 3, 1964.

Aristotle Onassis

Besides spending time with Bobby, Jackie also found companionship in Aristotle Onassis. He was a Greek billionaire whom she had met a few years earlier through her sister, Lee.

At first the two were friends, but the relationship turned romantic. Jackie introduced Onassis to her mother and stepfather. They did not approve. Onassis was twenty-three years older than Jackie. And he was Greek Orthodox, not Catholic. To make matters worse, Bobby did not like Onassis, either.

Eventually, Jackie's parents were won over by Onassis's kindness. But Bobby's feelings did not change. He was getting ready to run for president and asked Jackie to keep her relationship with Onassis a secret until after the election. Jackie agreed.

On June 5, 1968, Bobby Kennedy had just won a primary election in California. This brought him one step closer to becoming the Democratic nominee for president.

But after giving a victory speech, he was shot in the head by a man named Sirhan Sirhan. Bobby Kennedy died the next day.

Jackie was terrified. Her children's father had been shot and killed. Now their uncle was dead. She no longer felt it was safe for her family to live in the United States. She turned to Onassis, who could provide her with security, both financial and physical—he had private security guards. Jackie found him kind and smart and funny. They had already been discussing marriage, and now she decided this was the right decision.

On October 20, 1968, Jackie married Aristotle Onassis on his private island in Greece. Aristotle's two children from a previous marriage, Alexander and Christina, were not there. They objected to the marriage. And so did many Americans. One newspaper headline read "Jackie, How Could You?" Many people felt that Onassis was much too old for Jackie.

Others disagreed with Onassis's lifestyle. And still others felt that Jackie was disrespecting her husband's memory by marrying Onassis.

Jackie did not move her family to Greece full-time. Caroline and John Jr. stayed in New York City to attend school. Jackie spent part of the year in Greece, learning about the culture and language. Aristotle—who was known as Ari—lived on his yacht, or in his apartment in Paris. At times, he traveled with Jackie to New York.

Even with security guards, Jackie was still hounded by the press. Sometimes she wore large, dark sunglasses and a kerchief around her head to try to go unnoticed. But she was usually spotted,

and photographers snapped her photos. Americans still wanted to know about Jackie's every move.

Then on January 23, 1973, Alexander Onassis was killed in a plane crash. Devastated by the loss of his son, Ari never truly recovered. He and Jackie spent more and more time apart. And when they were together, Ari did not treat Jackie very well. Sometimes he yelled at her in front of guests. There were rumors about his romances with other women. As always, Jackie kept her emotions to herself. She would never show sadness or anger.

On March 15, 1975, Aristotle Onassis died. Forty-six-year-old Jackie was again a widow.

CHAPTER 9
Remembering Jackie

Jackie had to start her life again. She was back in New York City. Her children were now teenagers and didn't need her as much as they had when they were younger. One day, a friend suggested that Jackie find a job. At first Jackie wasn't sure. She hadn't had a paying job in so many years. But then she was offered a job as a book editor at

Viking Press. Jackie loved books. She said yes!

Jackie was a good editor. She worked hard and stayed at Viking for about two years, working on books about history and art—two subjects that she loved. Jackie's next job was with Doubleday Publishers. She stayed there for seventeen years. She made her own calls and typed her own  letters, rather than using a secretary. She attended office parties and was well liked and respected by her coworkers. And she edited many best-selling books, including *Blood Memory*, by the famous dancer Martha Graham; and *Fireworks: A History and Celebration*, by George Plimpton.

Jackie also had a passion for architecture. She said, "We are the only country in the world that trashes its old buildings. Too late we realize how very much we need them." Jackie tried to protect some of America's most beautiful buildings from destruction. She wrote petitions, staged protests, and helped raise money, all in the name of preserving history.

Jackie also tried to keep Jack's memory alive in any way she could. She helped create the John F. Kennedy Library and Museum, which opened in 1979 in Boston.

Grand Central Terminal

When this train station in New York City opened in 1871, it was filled with bronze and stone carvings, marble halls, and majestic stone archways. In 1967, Grand Central received landmark status, which meant that the building had special historical value to New York City and could not be torn down or altered. But by this time, the station had fallen on hard times. The place was dangerous and depressing.

Its once beautiful ceiling was now covered with soot. The roof leaked. The windows were painted black. Then a builder proposed to erect a fifty-five-story tower on top of the terminal. Many, including Jackie Kennedy, were opposed to this. In 1975, Jackie Kennedy helped form the Committee to Save Grand Central. The committee's efforts worked, saving and restoring this beautiful historic building.

In her personal life, Jackie began dating businessman Maurice Tempelsman. Like Jackie, he was also a private person. He understood Jackie and offered her stability and love. Yet the two

Maurice Tempelsman

never married because, although separated from his wife, Maurice was not divorced.

In December 1993, Maurice and Jackie traveled to the Caribbean for a vacation. Jackie fell ill, and they returned home. Two months later, a devastating announcement came—Jackie had cancer.

Determined to fight the disease, Jackie remained hopeful and cheerful, even through painful treatments. And as her condition grew worse, she continued to work. But soon, there was nothing more her doctors could do; Jackie was dying.

Jackie took to her bed in her apartment on Fifth Avenue in New York City, surrounded by friends and family. Outside her building, hordes of reporters gathered. Hundreds of well-wishers also stood there and prayed.

At 10:15 p.m., on Thursday, May 19, 1994, Jacqueline Bouvier Kennedy Onassis died. "My mother died surrounded by her friends and her family and her books, and the people and things that she loved. She did it in her own way, and on her own terms, and we all feel lucky for that," John Jr. said.

Jackie's funeral and burial were simple. A service was held at the same church in New York City where she was christened as a baby. Then, her body was flown to Washington, DC, to be laid to rest at Arlington National Cemetery, next to President Kennedy.

Jackie Kennedy will be remembered as a woman who always treated people with respect, a woman who valued culture, art, and the beautiful things life has to offer. Family was most important to her, and she cared for and loved her children and grandchildren up until the day she died. Even after her death, Jackie received many honors. A high school in New York City was named the Jacqueline Kennedy Onassis High School for International Careers. The reservoir in New York's Central Park also was renamed in her honor.

Caroline Kennedy

Growing up in the White House, Caroline was the darling of the media. The press loved to snap pictures of her playing outside or riding her pony. After her father's assassination, Caroline attended private school in New York City, and then Radcliffe College. She thought about becoming a photojournalist, but then decided to go to law school at Columbia University. On July 19, 1986, Caroline married Edwin Schlossberg. Like her mother, Caroline wanted her wedding to be a private affair— but it wasn't! A huge crowd stood outside the church on Cape Cod where the couple wed. Caroline and

Edwin have three children—Rose, Tatiana, and John. Caroline practiced law, worked with many charities as well as the New York City Department of Education, and also became an author. One of the books she helped create was *The Best-Loved Poems of Jacqueline Kennedy Onassis*. In 2013, President Barack Obama named Caroline the US ambassador to Japan.

John Fitzgerald Kennedy Jr.

Like his sister, John grew up in the eye of the media. He attended Brown University, where he became interested in many issues, such as gun control and civil rights. After graduation, John worked at various New York City government jobs. He then got a law degree from New York University.

In 1995, John co-founded *George* magazine, which focused on everything from politics to fashion.

Tall and handsome, John was often in the headlines, dating model Cindy Crawford and actresses Sarah Jessica Parker and Daryl Hannah. John finally settled down and married Carolyn Bessette at a private ceremony on Cumberland Island, Georgia, on September 21, 1996. On July 16, 1999, John piloted a plane carrying Carolyn and her sister Lauren to a family wedding on Martha's Vineyard, Massachusetts. Tragically, the plane crashed, killing all three.

With her grace, charm, talent, and intelligence, Jackie Kennedy captivated the world. And the world will always remember her.

Timeline of Jacqueline Kennedy's Life

1929	Born to Janet and John Bouvier in Southampton, New York
1933	Sister, Caroline Lee, is born
1947	Enters Vassar College
1950	Transfers to Georgetown University for senior year
1951	Starts working at the *Washington Times-Herald*
1953	Marries John Fitzgerald Kennedy in Newport, Rhode Island
1957	Daughter, Caroline, is born
1960	Son, John Fitzgerald Kennedy Jr., is born
1961	John F. Kennedy becomes president, and Jacqueline becomes First Lady
	Meets Soviet leader Nikita Khrushchev in Vienna
1962	Gives a television tour of the White House
1963	John F. Kennedy assassinated in Dallas, Texas
1964	Moves family to New York City
1968	Robert F. Kennedy assassinated in Los Angeles, California
	Marries Aristotle Onassis
1977	Begins work as an editor at Doubleday
1994	Diagnosed with cancer
	Dies at home in New York City

Timeline of the World

1929	The stock market crashes and the Great Depression begins
1931	Empire State Building is completed
1932	Amelia Earhart becomes the first woman to fly solo over the Atlantic Ocean
1941	Pearl Harbor bombed by Japan; America enters World War II
	Cheerios first introduced
1947	*The Diary of a Young Girl*, by Anne Frank, published
1955	Rosa Parks, a black woman, refuses to give up her seat on a bus in Montgomery, Alabama
1957	Sputnik sent into orbit by the Soviet Union
1964	Civil Rights Act passed in the United States
1965	Miniskirt first appears
1968	Martin Luther King Jr. assassinated
1974	US president Richard Nixon resigns
1975	Tennis player Arthur Ashe becomes the first black man to win Wimbledon
1979	Mother Teresa awarded the Nobel Peace Prize
1981	Sandra Day O'Connor becomes the first woman appointed to the US Supreme Court
1982	Michael Jackson releases *Thriller*
1985	Wreck of the *Titanic* found
1994	Nelson Mandela elected president of South Africa

Bibliography

* Books for young readers

*Agins, Donna Brown. *Jacqueline Kennedy Onassis: Legendary First Lady*. Berkeley Heights, NJ: Enslow Publishers, 2004.

Anderson, Christopher. *These Few Precious Days: The Final Year of Jack with Jackie*. New York: Gallery Books.

Cassidy, Tina. *Jackie After O*. New York: HarperCollins, 2012.

*McDonough, Yona Zeldis. *Who Was John F. Kennedy?* New York: Grosset & Dunlap, 2004.

*Stine, Megan. *Where Is the White House?* New York: Grosset & Dunlap, 2015.

31901066553191